The Curse of Tutankhamen

by Lou Eschle

Lucent Books, P.O. Box 289011, San Diego, CA 92198-9011

To my son Andy and my friend Terry

These and other titles are included in the Exploring the Unknown series:

> The Curse of Tutankhamen
> The Extinction of the Dinosaurs
> Haunted Houses

Library of Congress Cataloging-in-Publication Data
Eschle, Lou, 1940–
    The curse of Tutankhamen / by Lou Eschle.
        p. cm.—(Exploring the unknown)
    Includes bibliographical references and index.
    Summary: Explores conflicting theories about the unusual number of
deaths following the opening of King Tut's tomb in 1922.
    ISBN 1-56006-152-9 (alk. paper)
    1. Tutankhamen, King of Egypt—Tomb—Juvenile literature.
2. Egypt—Antiquities—Juvenile literature. 3. Blessing and
cursing—Juvenile literature. [1. Tutankhamen, King of Egypt—
Tomb. 2. Egypt—Antiquities. 3. Blessing and cursing.]
I. Title. II. Series: Exploring the unknown (San Diego, Calif.)
DT87.5.E85   1994
932'.014'092—dc20   93-4297
                                                                                  CIP
                                                                                  AC

Printed in the USA

CONTENTS

Mystery Beneath the Sand

The place was Egypt. The year was 1922. In appearance, it could have been almost any year in the long history of this area. The climate remains hot and dry. The people and their way of living have changed little in several centuries.

One other aspect of this land also remains the same. People are still digging. They are looking for tombs, searching for the burial places of those who once ruled this great land. For indeed, Egypt was one of the first great empires, and much history and treasure lie beneath its sand.

Temple of Hatshepsut at Luxor, the Valley of the Kings in Egypt. This valley is a treasure trove of ancient pharaohs' tombs and monuments. One of them belonged to Tutankhamen.

The cartouche of Tutankhamen. A cartouche is an oval or oblong figure containing a ruler's name. In this case, Tutankhamen's name is spelled with hieroglyphs.

What made 1922 a special year was a great discovery and the beginning of a great mystery. The discovery was the ancient tomb of a young Egyptian king. The mystery is the many deaths connected to the tomb's discovery. In the years following the opening of King Tutankhamen's tomb in the Nile River valley, more than three dozen people connected to its finding died sudden, mysterious deaths. Some say the deaths were mere coincidence. But others say they were caused by a powerful ancient curse.

CHAPTER 1

The Carter-Carnarvon Expedition

In November 1922, British archaeologist Howard Carter was leading a group searching for ancient artifacts. Carter's patron, Lord Carnarvon, had funded this expedition to the Valley of the Kings. Carnarvon had one of the world's largest collections of Egyptian antiquities, and he wanted to add to it. Carter and his crew were searching for one particular tomb in this desolate place—the tomb of King Tutankhamen. They had searched for it for seven years. But this was to be the last digging season. Carnarvon had had enough of Egypt. He had been coming here since 1903. But since the end of World War I, revolution had been stirring in Egypt. The British had ruled Egypt for many years. Now the native population wanted its freedom. The threat of revolt made Lord Carnarvon uneasy.

Lord Carnarvon, a British collector of Egyptian artifacts and the financial backer of Howard Carter's expeditions. Carnarvon's sudden death from a mysterious fever fueled reports about "the mummy's curse."

Howard Carter needed to make a big discovery. This would keep Carnarvon's interest alive and his money flowing. Without Carnarvon's money, Carter could not do his work.

In the previous seven years, Carter's diggers had found little to reward Carnarvon's interest, or Carter's own. Now Carter was under great pressure. Carnarvon wanted a prize, regardless of the consequences—and there would be some: Carnarvon would soon die mysteriously. So would many others connected with this expedition. Perhaps, some say, they were victims of the curse of Tutankhamen.

A Splendid Discovery

Howard Carter first came to Egypt in 1890. He was eighteen years old and the son of a well-known English painter. His first job was to sketch the carvings and reliefs that were found on temple walls. In the 1890s photography was a young art. Cameras were large and awkward. That is why drawings were the main way records were made of things like this. During this period Carter was considered the most talented artist in Egypt. He was much sought after for his abilities.

At age twenty-five he was named Inspector General of the Monuments in Upper Egypt. His task was to protect the historic tombs from robbers. He took his job very seriously.

On one occasion he found a newly discovered tomb that had been ransacked by thieves. He was determined to catch the grave robbers. After making plaster casts of their footprints, he hired a desert tracker. Just as in stories about the Wild West, the trackers traced the footprints to the home of the thieves. There they found the evidence they were looking for and brought the crooks to trial.

In 1907 Carter and Lord Carnarvon had become partners in the quest to find traces of ancient Egypt. For many years Carter had been digging in the Valley of the Kings, but he had made few important discoveries. Carter was beginning to believe little was left here to find. Then, on November 4, 1922, a strange quiet settled over the pit where he and his crew were working.

"By the solemn silence all around caused by the stoppage of work, I guessed that something out of the usual had occurred," he later wrote. "My foreman was most cheerful, and confidentially told me that the beginning of a staircase had been discovered."

Howard Carter's artistic talents gained him a strong reputation in archaeological circles.

With remembered excitement he wrote,

It was a thrilling moment for an excavator [digger] in that valley of unutterable silence, quite alone save for his native staff and workmen, suddenly to find himself, after so many years of toilsome work, on the verge of what looked like a magnificent discovery.

And indeed it was a wonderful discovery. His crew had uncovered the first of sixteen steps that led to a doorway of plaster and brick. On the door was imprinted the stamp of the Royal Necropolis, or royal cemetery. The stamp showed the god Anubis, the magical protector of the burial chamber. Anubis had a black jackal head with two pointed ears. He stood above nine bound captives. These captives represented the nine enemies of Egypt. The presence of the unbroken seal suggested that Carter had made a rare find: an unviolated royal tomb.

The god Anubis, depicted with a jackal head. Anubis was the god of the dead and of embalming.

Carter's crew first discovered a step (right) and then the sealed entrance to Tutankhamen's tomb (left). These finds caused great excitement in Carter and his workers. At last they were near their goal!

Who Was Tutankhamen?

Who was Tutankhamen, the pharaoh whose fantastic tomb Howard Carter found?

Scholars have discovered that Tutankhamen was no long-lived king who led dynasties. In fact, Tutankhamen was only nine years old when he became pharaoh in 1334 B.C. He was called the Boy King. His reign lasted for only nine years.

Since he was so young, he was easily manipulated. A powerful group of court officials, priests, and generals actually ran the country during this time of great upheaval.

By 1325 B.C., eighteen-year-old Tutankhamen was old enough to assert himself. The powers behind the throne did not want to let this happen. Tutankhamen, the Boy King, was probably murdered. A modern autopsy done in the 1920s showed that his skull had a wound caused by a blow or fall.

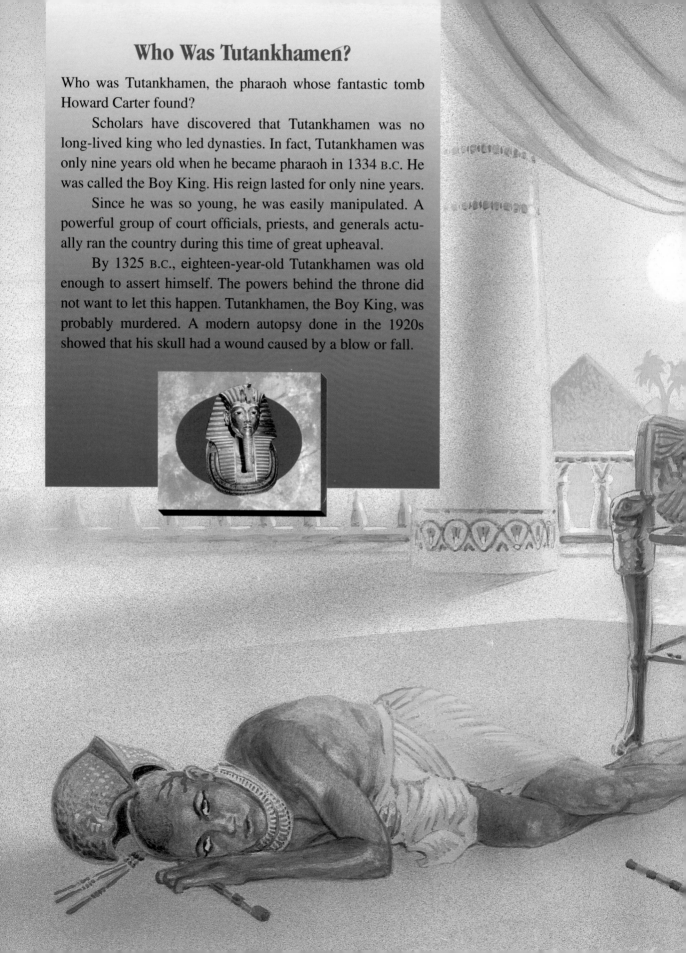

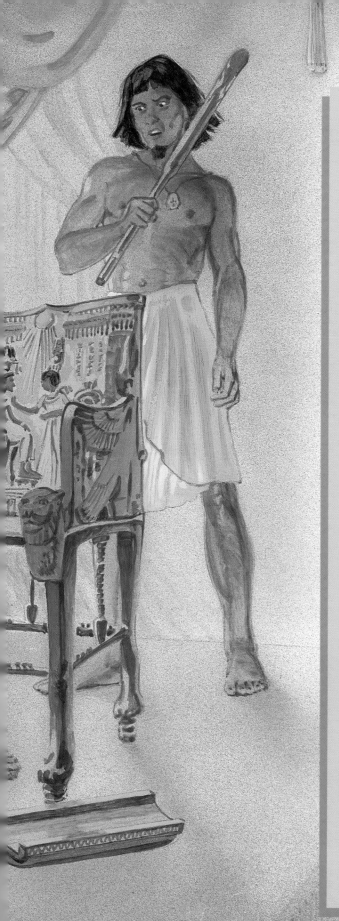

In Tut's Tomb

The ancient Egyptians believed their dead had to be well supplied for life after death. They commonly surrounded the dead person with his or her earthly possessions. The poor might have a few items, but royalty and the rich were surrounded by unequaled treasures.

King Tutankhamen's tomb is one of the few discovered by archaeologists that had not been badly violated by grave robbers. Archaeologists say that if such a minor king was buried with such lavish treasures, they can only imagine what might have been buried with more important pharaohs. Here are only a few of the thousands of things found in Tut's incredible tomb:

- Boats to take the king on trips through the heavens
- Weapons, including swords, spears, bows, and throw sticks to use against enemies in the afterlife
- An intricately carved golden throne
- Six magnificent full-sized chariots
- Many containers of precious oils or foods such as fruit, meat, wine, and bread
- Hundreds of statuettes of the king, called *ushabtis,* inscribed with the king's name and the name of the person who offered them; life-size statues of the king and his guards
- Ornate chests filled with clothing, shoes, and jewelry made of gold and semiprecious stones
- Household objects such as chairs, beds, and game boards
- And much, much more

Tut's tomb itself consisted of four massive shrines of gilded wood inlaid with semiprecious stones. Inside them a red stone coffin contained three nested mummy cases, the innermost made of 2,400 pounds of solid gold. And in the last of these cases was the mummy, wrapped with linen interlaced with jewels and amulets, and wearing the famous solid gold death mask.

Carter quickly sent a cable to Lord Carnarvon. It said, "At last have made a wonderful discovery in Valley; a magnificent tomb with seals intact; re-covered same for your arrival; congratulations."

The Tomb Is Opened

Carnarvon arrived from England twelve days later. He joined Carter at the site of the new discovery. On November 26 Carter described in his diary "the day of days, the most wonderful that I have ever lived through."

With great excitement, Howard Carter (left) and workers smash through the tomb's entrance.

Carter's crew bored a small hole in the upper left-hand corner of the door. Carter wrote, "Darkness and blank space, as far as an iron testing rod could reach, showed that whatever lay beyond was empty." He added,

> Widening the hole a little, I inserted the candle and peered in. . . . At first I could see nothing, the hot air escaping from the chamber causing the candle flame to flicker, but presently, as my eyes grew accustomed to the light, details of the room within emerged slowly from the mist, strange animals, statues and gold—everywhere the glint of gold.

Carter's pulse quickened. He recorded,

> For the moment—an eternity it must have seemed to the others standing by—I was struck dumb with amazement, and when Lord Carnarvon, unable to stand the suspense any longer, inquired anxiously, "Can you see anything?" it was all I could do to get out the words, Yes, wonderful things.

Howard Carter and Lord Carnarvon were about to realize a dream. They were about to enter the tomb of the pharaoh Tutankhamen.

Items from Tutankhamen's tomb. Among the treasures shown here are two of the huge, gilded, animal-shaped couches.

Breaking the Seal

A group of about two dozen people were present at the opening of Tutankhamen's tomb. Among them were the king of Egypt and the British high commissioner. The observers waited eagerly for Carter and Carnarvon to remove plaster and stones from a door to the inner chamber. This room would contain the coffin of the pharaoh. When this was done Carter was the first to hurry into the chamber. He wanted to find out if the coffin was intact. (Smashed jars and furniture in the outer rooms showed that tomb robbers had previously broken in and priests had later resealed the tomb.)

Detail from one of the highly carved and decorated chests found in the tomb. This shows Tutankhamen and his queen Ankhesenamun on a hunting expedition.

By the light of an electric lamp, Carter could see a large gilded shrine looming in front of him. The great golden structure almost filled the room that measured twenty-one feet by fifteen feet. Carter rushed to the doors of the shrine and pried them open. He could see that the seals to the chamber that held the coffin were intact. This meant that what lay beyond had not been seen by anyone for thousands of years.

Carter wrote,

I think at the moment we did not even want to break the seal, for a feeling of intrusion had descended heavily upon us with the opening of the doors, heightened, probably, by

Carter and Carnarvon in Tutankhamen's tomb, preparing some items for travel. The great gilded shrine that held Tutankhamen's mummy is in the background.

The gilded outermost coffin. Inside were nested two other mummy cases, one made of solid gold; then the wrapped mummy wearing the famous solid gold mask.

the almost painful impressiveness of a linen pall [fabric draped over a coffin], decorated with golden rosettes. . . . We felt that we were in the presence of the dead King and must do him reverence, and in imagination could see the doors of the successive shrines open one after the other till the innermost disclosed the King himself. Carefully, and as silently as possible, we re-closed the great swing doors.

Now Carnarvon and his men began to prepare for the removal of the king's coffin and the objects in the tomb. They readied packing crates and boxes.

But first Lord Carnarvon had to go to Cairo. He was negotiating with the Cairo museum over how the tomb's contents would be divided. Both the museum and Carnarvon wanted a share of what was found. Carnarvon had his own private collection and, of course, the museum wanted to retain a large number of the ancient Egyptian objects.

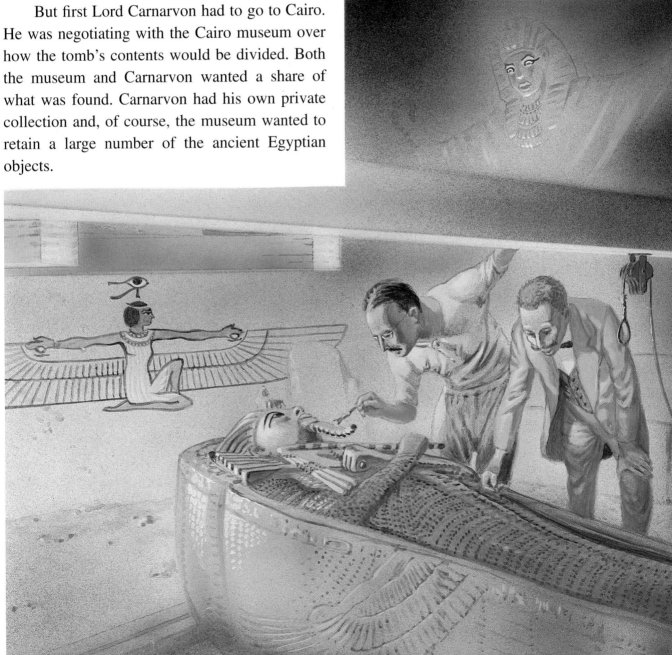

The explorers covered the opening of the tomb with debris. This was to prevent anyone from tampering with the tomb. They also posted guards. Carnarvon then went to Cairo, while Carter stayed near the excavations.

A few weeks later Carter received word that Carnarvon was ill with a high fever. The illness had started quite suddenly. Carnarvon had a temperature of 104 degrees and he shook with chills. After twelve days of this, Carter learned, Lord Carnarvon died. The cause of his death has been described in various ways. Some said it was an infection caused when he cut himself shaving. Others blamed an infection from a mosquito bite.

Still others said it was King Tut's curse.

CHAPTER 2

The Curse Strikes

When Lord Carnarvon died in 1923, the newspapers made the most of it. They began to talk about the curse of the pharaohs. They searched files to find other mysterious or unexplained deaths. Reporters were surprised to find so many odd deaths associated in some way with ancient tombs.

One of the strange deaths was that of Giovanni Belzoni in 1823. Belzoni was the Italian discoverer in 1817 of the tomb of Seti I, a pharaoh from the nineteenth dynasty (about 1300 B.C.). Belzoni had literally wallowed in mummies. This is what he wrote of his visit to the ruins of the ancient Egyptian city of Thebes where Seti I's tomb was found:

> Once I was conducted through a passage of about twenty feet in length and no wider than that a body could be forced through. It was choked with mummies and I could not pass without putting my face in contact with that of some decayed Egyptian; but as the passage inclined downwards, my own weight helped me on: however, I could not help being covered with bones, legs, arms, and heads rolling from above. Thus I proceeded from one cave to another, all full of mummies piled up in various ways, some standing, some lying and some on their heads.

Belzoni made a great deal of money in Europe selling the objects he unearthed in Egypt. With this money he financed another trip to Africa. But he never saw Egypt again.

His death occurred in Sierra Leone, in western Africa. Ravaged by a mysterious disease, he said, "I feel the hand of death upon me. . . . I only have a few hours to live and I know it." He died a short time later. He was forty-five years old.

Giovanni Battista Belzoni, Italian explorer and archaeologist. He wrote of his colorful and terrifying experiences in Egyptian tombs.

Some thought he died because he had robbed the ancient tombs that were protected by pharaohs' curses.

Another case was that of Theodor Bilharz. He was a German doctor and scientist who did autopsies, or medical examinations on mummies. His work enabled him to discover the cause of an illness that had plagued Egypt for thousands of years. The disease is now called Bilharzia, named in his honor.

In the summer of 1862, Dr. Bilharz made his last trip up the Nile. On the way to Cairo, he suffered from violent cramps and fell into a coma. He never regained consciousness. After two weeks he died. The official record said the cause of death was typhoid fever, but his colleagues disagreed. They said he was the victim of another mysterious disease. Others said he was killed by the pharaohs' curses.

Tomb of Seti I, a pharaoh who gained the throne about thirty years after Tutankhamen's death. Here, a surveyor takes measurements of the elaborately decorated tomb. It is typical of the time and expense lavished on a ruler's tomb.

More Mysterious Deaths

Edward Ayrton, an English archaeologist, also had a mysterious end. He had spent many years digging in Egypt. At the age of thirty-one he drowned while hunting in England. In 1911 Harold Jones was excavating a tomb in Egypt. Suddenly, he came down with a high fever and died after a short illness. Both of these deaths, many people claimed, were the result of ancient curses.

Many tragic events have been linked to the opening of Tutankhamen's tomb.

Some newspapers even blamed the sinking of the *Titanic* on the curse of the dead pharaohs. At the time it sank, the ship was said to be carrying the mummy of a high priestess of the eighteenth dynasty.

Reporters found many other strange cases that they could connect in some way to the tombs of long-dead pharaohs. Many could be directly related to the excavation of Tutankhamen's tomb.

Making a Mummy

Ancient Egyptians went to great pains to preserve their dead. They believed in life after death. They believed the body must be properly preserved for the afterlife.

The person who prepared the body slit the stomach lining of the dead person. He removed the soft organs and rubbed them with oils and perfumes. He placed them in separate compartments of a small casket, or chest. These would later be placed in the tomb with the mummified body. He drew the brain out through the nose with the help of a metal hook. He threw it away, for the Egyptians did not believe the brain was of great importance. The heart was left however, for it was thought to be the center of a person's intelligence. For seventy days the embalmer soaked the body in a kind of salt called natron. When the body was sufficiently dried out, he carefully wrapped it in strips of linen fabric. The mummy was now ready for the tomb.

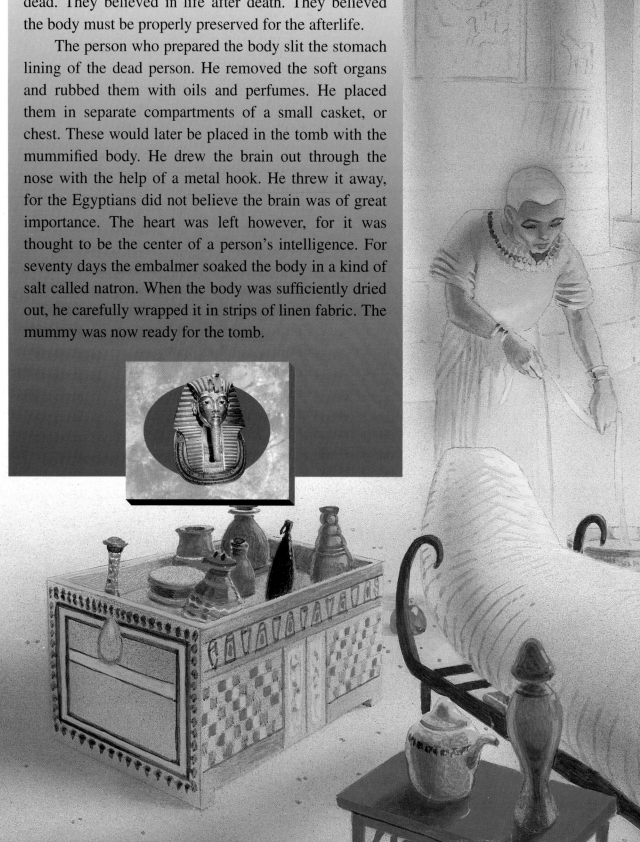

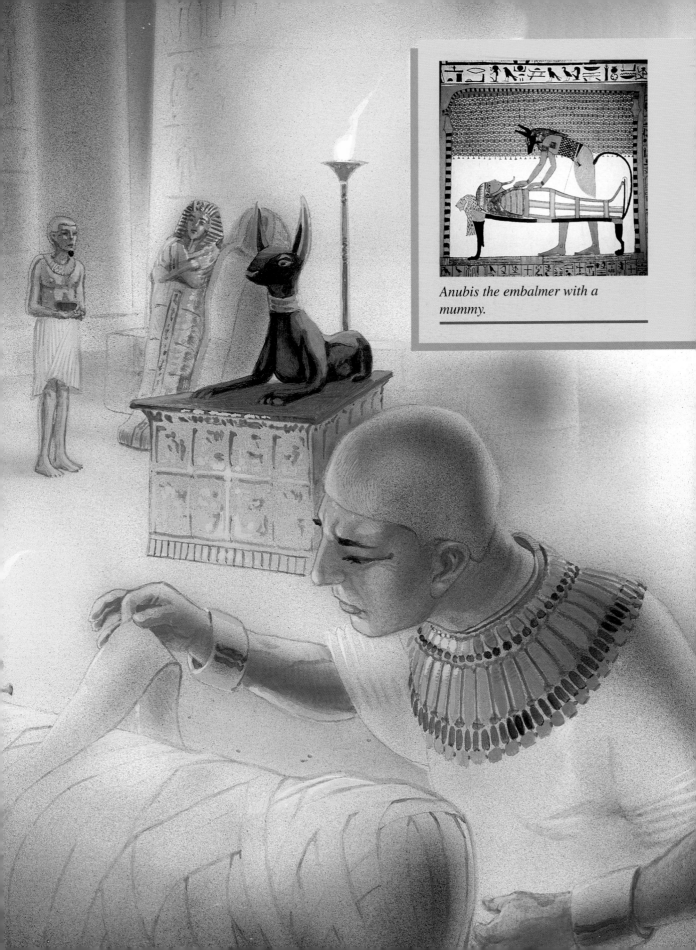

Anubis the embalmer with a mummy.

Arthur Mace was an American archaeologist from the University of Chicago. He had helped Carter and Carnarvon tear down the door to the inner chamber of the tomb. Shortly after Carnarvon's death, Mace began to complain of exhaustion. Doctors told him he had developed a bad case of tuberculosis. He left Egypt and headed for America, but he died soon afterward.

George Jay Gould, son of a famous American financial wizard, went to Egypt in 1923. Gould was a longtime friend of Carnarvon and was curious about the tomb. The morning after viewing it, Gould came down with a high fever. That evening he died. At first, doctors could not explain Gould's death. Later they concluded that he must have had bubonic plague, a dangerous and quick-acting disease. But many were not convinced by this explanation.

Another visitor to the excavation site was Joel Wool, a British businessman. He died from a high fever soon after he returned to England.

Archibald Douglas Reid, a famous British radiologist (a person who uses X rays to diagnose illnesses) also died mysteriously. He is the man who in 1922 cut the cords that were wound around Tut's mummy. He did this so that X rays of the corpse could be taken. Shortly after he finished his work, he developed a strange feebleness. He died in 1924 when he returned to England.

In 1925 Professor Douglas Derry and a chemist named Alfred Lucas performed an autopsy on King Tut's mummy. On November 11 the two men began to remove the linen fabric that wrapped the body. They found 143 pieces of jewelry wound in the wrappings. They also found several amulets, or charms against evil or injury, as they removed the strips of linen.

This miniature coffin is one of four that held Tutankhamen's internal organs. It is as elaborately made as the full-size mummy cases. It is made of beaten gold inlaid with colored glass and carnelian, a semiprecious stone.

These amulets included a symbol of the goddess Isis, two gold pendents representing the god Osiris, and stones with the likenesses of various other gods. The amulets were believed to have two purposes: to protect the pharaoh on his journey to the world of the dead, and to curse anyone who would interrupt his peace.

Soon after the autopsy Alfred Lucas died of a heart attack. A short time later, Professor Derry developed a disorder of his circulation system and also died.

By 1929 twenty-two people who were involved in some way with the opening of King Tutankhamen's grave were dead. Of this number,

Treasures from Tutankhamen's tomb. The amulet and necklace are both made of gold inlaid with semiprecious stones. Their designs include many symbols important to the Egyptians. The scarab, or beetle, represents the sun god raising the sun in the sky at dawn.

some sources said, thirteen had been present at the opening of the inner chamber. One was Carter's secretary Richard Bethell, who died of sudden collapse of his circulatory system.

Widespread Effects of the Curse

Strange events associated with Bethell's death seemed to suggest that the curse could reach beyond those directly involved with Tut's tomb. When Bethell's father, Lord Westbury, heard of his son's death, he jumped from the seventh floor of his London house. Then, on the way to Lord Westbury's funeral, the hearse ran over a small boy.

Science and King Tut's Curse

This alabaster cup found in Tutankhamen's tomb is called the wishing cup. The hieroglyphics are a message wishing the young pharaoh a long and happy life.

W hat was the curse that many feared had caused so many mysterious deaths?

The pharaohs and priests of early Egypt had many reasons to encourage a belief in curses. The main one related to their ideas about death. They believed that when people died the gods judged them. If found worthy, they would forever have an afterlife. The afterlife would be similar in many ways to life on earth. Therefore, the ancient Egyptians buried their dead with possessions that would be useful to them in the afterlife. These included food, clothing, furniture, military equipment, riches, and even pets and slaves. These treasures offered many temptations to thieves.

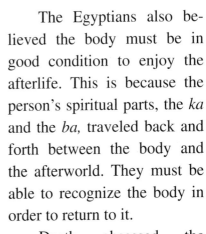

The Egyptians also believed the body must be in good condition to enjoy the afterlife. This is because the person's spiritual parts, the *ka* and the *ba,* traveled back and forth between the body and the afterworld. They must be able to recognize the body in order to return to it.

Death obsessed the Egyptians. Their greatest fear was that their corpses would be destroyed. This would destroy their chance for eternal life. It is not surprising, therefore, that they used every means, material and magical, to protect the tombs. They preserved bodies through mummification. They carved the walls and doors of the burial chamber with prayers, as well as with threats or curses. As the priests sealed the tomb of a dead pharaoh, they might say, "I have set ablaze all the area around me; the flames will seize any person who comes near me with hostile intent."

Some say Howard Carter's crew uncovered a tablet with another curse: "Death comes on wings to he who enters the tomb of a pharaoh." The tablet, however, if it ever existed, has disappeared. No evidence of it remains.

The ancient priests hoped their prayers and curses would keep grave robbers from disturbing the pharaohs' tombs and harming their bodies.

Ancient Egyptians believed a dead person's heart would be weighed by the gods to determine the person's worthiness for the afterlife. This papyrus painting portrays Egyptian gods and the scale used to weigh the heart.

The Grave Robbers

For centuries, grave robbers broke into the ancient Egyptian tombs. Their carelessness destroyed many treasures and they stole many more.

Sadly, none of these precautions worked. The fear of divine retribution did keep most people away from the tombs. But the lure of fabulous wealth or fame overcame many people's common sense or superstition. Even some pharaohs ignored the warnings and took over the tombs of their predecessors. Pinejem I, who died in 997 B.C., used the coffin of Thutmosis I, who had died five hundred years earlier.

One story tells of a grave robber in the late 1800s who used the superstitions about pharaohs' curses to his advantage. He and two other robbers discovered a hole in the ground. His companions lowered him into the hole, and he found himself in a cavern with many mummies and their burial goods. But when his friends pulled him up, he said the hole had been empty.

Later, he brought a donkey to the hole, killed it, and pushed it in. The donkey's body rotted. Most people thought the smell from the carcass, or dead body, was the smell of

Today's scientists use sophisticated tools to learn more about the past. Here, an art restorer at the Boston Museum of Fine Arts prepares a mummy for a CAT scan.

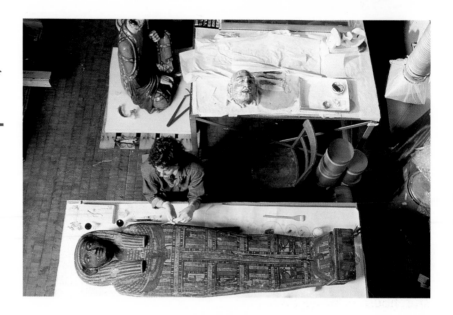

demons. This was enough to keep the local people away, and the grave robber was able to steal from the site for years. He was finally caught when some of the jewels and other antiquities he was selling illegally were traced back to him.

Not all of those who disturbed the ancient graves were thieves seeking precious treasure to sell for profit. Modern "grave robbers" include archaeologists, scientists who hope to learn about the past by studying its remains. Most of these people do not believe in pharaohs' curses. James Breasted, for example, was a well-known archaeologist in the early 1900s. He heard many strange noises when he was working in Tutankhamen's tomb. He figured out logical reasons for them. He wrote this after working in the tomb:

> As I labored, surrounded on all sides by stacks of ancient objects, I became aware of a strange rustling. Murmuring, whispering sounds rose and fell. These erratic [irregular] fluttering sounds were caused by the slow physical changes that were taking place in the objects. Taking down the plastered outer doors to the chambers had broken the air-tight sealing of the tomb. The stable sterile environment had been broken. After thousands of years of slow physical change and chemical interaction with the atmosphere of the tomb the balance had been tipped by the intrusion of the archaeologists. All the objects in the tomb were dry beyond belief.

Breasted's logical explanations, however, do not explain the many mysterious deaths that occurred.

Science Enters the Picture

Can there really be anything to King Tut's curse? Is it possible that the priests of ancient Egypt could affect people centuries later with what they knew of magic or science? Today we know that over thousands of years the priests of Egypt experimented with both. Perhaps the priests thought curses would not be enough to discourage those who would disturb the tombs of kings. The priests may have added science to their storehouse of protection.

The powerful priests had accumulated vast amounts of knowledge in many areas of science. They recorded their knowledge in thousands of books. Tragically, the fire that consumed the great library at Alexandria destroyed most of these books. This happened during the reign of Cleopatra. Archaeologists and scholars have found a few glimpses of the knowledge these books contained. Scraps of ancient parchment and clay tablets give just a hint of what the ancient Egyptians knew.

Egyptian priests using their knowledge of poisons and magic to concoct formulas that will harm or kill grave robbers.

The Mummy's Hand

Professor Brian Emery was an Egyptologist. One night he was camped at the site where he had been working. Around his tent were tables on which lay the mummies he had found during the day. Suddenly, from inside his tent, Emery heard a sound. He looked up and a mummy hand appeared. It grabbed the tent flap and slowly drew it open. Emery froze in shock and fear. He thought he knew better, but now he wondered: Was it possible that one of the ancient mummies had come to life to seek revenge for being disturbed?

The hand finally stopped moving. After a time, Emery calmed down enough to go outside to investigate. He discovered that one of the tables had collapsed. The mummy on it had fallen, and its hand had caught in the tent flap.

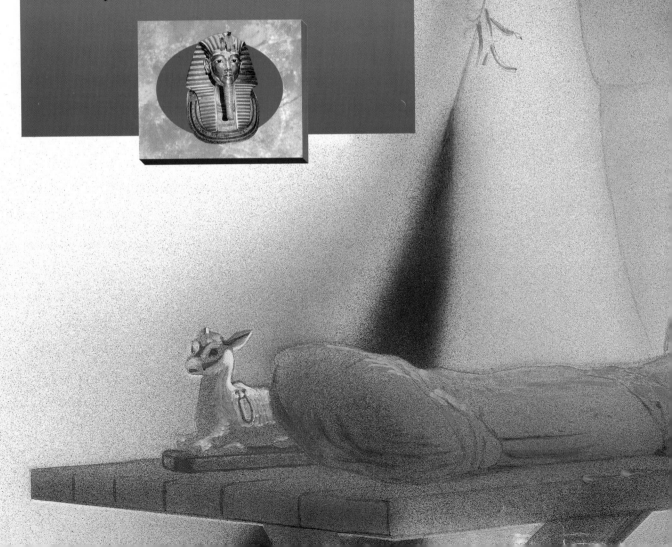

Poison

The god Horus, in the shape of a falcon, delivers a captive to King Narmer, thought to be another name for King Menes. Here the king is about to strike the captive with a club, but Menes also had the knowledge to kill with poisons.

One area in which the priests were experts was the field of drugs. They used drugs, often in the form of herbs or extractions from them, for medical purposes as well as for religious ceremonies. Egypt, a trading nation, had access to the potions and cures used by the surrounding peoples. For example, it imported resins, such as incense and myrrh, from Mesopotamia, a land known today as Iraq. Resins are juices from trees and plants. Ancient people used many of them for curing and preserving items that could rot.

It should not surprise us that the Egyptians also knew a lot about poisons. The first pharaoh, Menes, grew poisonous plants in his garden. He kept careful records of their effects. Arsenic, hemlock, henbane, and opium were all known and used by the priests and pharaohs. Cleopatra was said to have known how to mix poisons expertly. She learned the mixtures from ancient writings. Occasionally she tested these poisons on her slaves. Her lover, the Roman commander Mark Antony, was not totally comfortable with what she knew about poisons. He ate with Cleopatra only when a food taster was present.

The Egyptians learned that some poisons need to be ingested—eaten, drunk, or inhaled—to harm their victims. Others need to penetrate the skin. Still others need only to contact the skin to kill their victims. Modern chemical analyses reveal that poisons were sometimes mixed into the paints used on tomb walls and artifacts. Arsenic, aconite, and conium are just a few that have been found. Did the priests put poisons in the paints in the hope that anyone who dared to disturb a pharaoh's tomb would come into contact with them and die? Chemists have found that even when the drugs are dry and ancient many of them keep their strength.

The Bible also mentions the use of poison by the ancient Egyptians. The fourth book of Moses, for example, describes a test for women accused of adultery. If a woman refused to admit guilt, she was to be taken to the temple. There she would be given poisoned water. If she survived, which few did, she was found innocent because she was believed to be protected by God's grace. If she was guilty, the poison would kill her. For the Egyptians described by Moses, the poisoned water acted as a lie detector and also as the judge and executioner.

Scorpion bites are poisonous and fairly common in Egypt. The symptoms include muscle cramps, weak pulse, breathing problems, and finally paralysis. The Egyptians knew this. Proof is in the medical parchments that recommended honey and hippopotamus excrement (body waste) as a cure. Is it possible that the ancient priests found a way to use scorpion poison to kill the grave robbers of the future?

Insect and snake poisons were recently studied in Paris. Dr. M. Martiny found that drying these poisons does not decrease their strength. Not even a major change in temperature affects the strength of cobra venom. Perhaps the ancient priests were also aware of this.

Howard Carter spent much of his life in the tombs of pharaohs. He lived to be sixty-six and died in 1939. He spent much

A cobra (top) and scorpion (bottom). The ancient priests may have been able to preserve the poisons from these deadly desert beasts in a form that would kill or sicken grave robbers.

Is it possible that poisonous substances placed inside Tutankhamen's tomb were responsible for some of the mysterious deaths?

of his life in pain. He often suffered from attacks of dizziness and weakness. His suffering included hallucinations and frequent headaches. All these can be symptoms of poisoning.

Fungus

Archaeologists have long known of a strange illness called the Coptic Itch. It takes the form of skin rashes and difficult breathing. Its symptoms are also similar to those of pneumonia. Scholars believe Coptic Itch is caused by a fungus. Some believe this is the cause of the pharaoh's curse. But is the fungus hardy enough to survive in burial chambers for three or four thousand years?

Arthur Mace was a noted archaeologist. He reported that the walls of Tutankhamen's tomb were covered with a strange fungus. Could this have been the cause of the deaths? In 1903 Lord Carnarvon had suffered from a lung infection. A pneumonia-like disease caused by a fungus might affect someone like him, already weakened by an illness.

What's the Answer?

Poison and fungus are two of the possible explanations some scientists offer for the "curse" of King Tutankhamen's tomb. Others have suggested radioactive rocks or deadly bacteria. Still others say the deaths related to Tut's tomb are mere coincidence. So far, no one knows for sure.

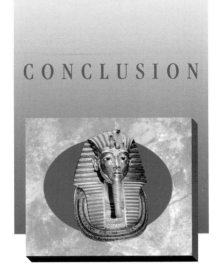

The Search Goes On

The priests of ancient Egypt had many ways to stop or punish those who disturbed the tombs of their pharaohs. But was their knowledge strong enough to kill centuries later? Many deaths connected with the discovery of King Tut's tomb cannot be explained by science. Maybe they never will be.

People have to decide for themselves if they believe in the ancient curse or not. If there *is* something to it, this author hopes the curse does not extend to those who write about it—or to those who read about it!

DEATH COMES ON WINGS TO HE WHO ENTERS THE TOMB OF A PHARAOH

Deaths and Survivals

Authors James Hamilton-Paterson and Carol Andrews report that the Curator of Egyptology at the Metropolitan Museum in New York wanted to find out if King Tut's curse was real.

In 1934 he did a study to determine how many people had been affected by the "curse." He found that of the twenty-six people present at the opening of the tomb, six had died within ten years. Twenty-two people had viewed the opening of Tut's coffin. Only two of them were dead ten years later. Ten people had been present when Tut's mummy was unwrapped in 1925. The curator said all of them were still alive in 1934. The curator concluded that the "curse" was a fraud.

However, in 1972 the curse was in the news again. Dr. Gamal Hehrez, head of the Cairo museum, prepared Tutankhamen's golden mask for travel to London. Reporters asked if he believed in the curse. He replied that he did not. Four weeks later, he died suddenly of circulatory collapse.

Lord Carnarvon's son was in New York in 1977 for an exhibit of artifacts from King Tut's tomb. Asked about the curse, he told an interviewer, "I neither believe it nor disbelieve it, but I would not accept a million pounds [British money] to enter the tomb of Tutankhamen."

Glossary

Some of the following words have more than one meaning. The meaning given here is the one used in this book.

afterlife: Life after death, which the ancient Egyptians believed would be very similar to the life they knew.

amulet: Charm or ornament, often inscribed with a magic saying to protect the wearer against evil.

antiquities: Old or ancient objects, such as vases and jewelry.

Anubis: Egyptian god of death; takes the form of a jackal.

archaeologist: A person who studies past human life and activities by studying their remains, such as ancient ruined buildings and monuments, bones, and pieces of pottery.

artifact: An object representing a particular culture, such as a tool, a pot, or an item of clothing.

autopsy: Detailed medical examination of a dead body to determine cause of death and other things.

ba: A person's individual character or spirit; early Egyptians believed it survived physical death.

circulatory disease: Illness affecting the blood, blood vessels, or heart.

corpse: Dead body.

dynasty: A group of rulers, generally descended from the same person.

Egyptologist: A person who studies Egyptian antiquities.

excavate: To dig out.

Isis: Egyptian nature god; wife and sister of Osiris.

ka: A sort of invisible spiritual twin. Ancient Egyptians believed it survived death and lived in much the same manner the person had lived on earth—eating, drinking, working, and so on. It used the food and belongings left in the person's tomb.

mummy: A preserved body, especially one preserved by the ancient Egyptians.

necropolis: Cemetery.

Osiris: Egyptian god of the world of the dead.

patron: A person who supports or pays for the work of another.

pharaoh: A ruler of ancient Egypt.

radiologist: A doctor specializing in the use of X rays.

relief: A three-dimensional wall painting in which the details have been sculpted to stand out from the flat surface.

retribution: Repayment, especially for a crime or an offense.

seal: The wax or plaster symbol that symbolically closes a tomb.

Valley of the Kings: A place near the Nile River in Egypt that houses the tombs of many Egyptian pharaohs.

For Further Reading

Aliki, *Mummies Made in Egypt*. New York: Harper and Row, 1979.

Daniel Cohen, *The Tomb Robbers*. New York: McGraw-Hill, 1980.

A. Rosalie David, *The Egyptian Kingdoms*. Oakland, CA: Equinox, 1988.

I. E. S. Edwards, *Tutankhamun: His Tomb and Treasures*. New York: Alfred A. Knopf, 1976.

Shirley Glubok, *Discovering Tut-ankh-Amen's Tomb*. New York: Macmillan, 1968.

George Hart, *Eyewitness Books: Ancient Egypt*. New York: Alfred A. Knopf, 1990.

Nancy Jenkins, *The Boat Beneath the Pyramids*. New York: Holt, Rinehart, Winston, 1980.

Patricia Lauber, *Tales Mummies Tell*. New York: Thomas Y. Crowell, 1980.

Ange-Pierre Leca, *The Egyptian Way of Death*. Garden City, NY: Doubleday, 1981.

Arnold Madison, *Mummies in Fact and Fiction*. New York: Franklin Watts, 1980.

Barbara Mitchell, *Great Mysteries/Opposing Viewpoints: Pyramids*. San Diego: Greenhaven Press, 1988.

Mildred Pace, *Wrapped for Eternity*. New York: McGraw-Hill, 1974.

Liz Payne, *The Pharaohs of Ancient Egypt*. New York: Random House/Landmark, 1964.

Lila Perl, *Mummies, Tombs, and Treasure: Secrets of Ancient Egypt*. New York: Clarion Books, 1987.

Nicholas Reeves, *Into the Mummy's Tomb: The Real-Life Discovery of Tutankhamen's Treasures*. New York: Scholastic/Madison Press, 1992.

Miriam Stead, *Egyptian Life*. Cambridge, MA: Harvard University Press, 1986.

Irene Swinburne, *Behind the Sealed Door: The Discovery of the Tomb and Treasures of Tutankhamun*. New York: Sniffen Court Books, 1977.

Works Consulted

Cyril Aldred, *The Egyptians*. New York: Thames and Hudson, 1961.

Howard Carter, *The Tomb of Tutankhamen*. New York: E. P. Dutton, 1972.

Michael Carter, *Tutankhamun: The Golden Monarch*. New York: David McKay, 1972.

Christine Desroches-Noblecourt, *Tutankhamen: Life and Death of a Pharaoh*. New York: New York Graphic Society, 1963.

Christine El Mahdy, *Mummies: Myth and Magic in Ancient Egypt*. New York: Thames and Hudson, 1989.

James Hamilton-Patterson and Carol Andrews, *Mummies: Death and Life in Ancient Egypt*. New York: Viking, 1979.

James E. Harris and Kent R. Weeks, *X-Raying the Pharaohs*. New York: Charles Scribner's Sons, 1973.

T. G. H. James, *Excavating in Egypt*. Chicago: University of Chicago Press, 1982.

T. G. H. James, *Pharaoh's People*. North Pomfret, VT: Trafalgar Press/The Bodley Head, 1984.

Pierre Montet, *Lives of the Pharaohs*. Cleveland: World Publishing, 1968.

John Romer, *Ancient Lives: Daily Life in Egypt of the Pharaohs*. New York: Holt, Rinehart, Winston, 1984.

John Romer, *Valley of the Kings*. New York: Henry Holt, 1981.

Philip Vandenberg, *The Curse of the Pharaohs*. New York: Lippincott, 1975.

John Anthony West, *Ancient Egypt*. Alfred A. Knopf, 1985.

Index

Credits

Picture

Cover photo by Werner Forman/Art Resource, NY

The Bettmann Archive, 18 (top)

Boltin Picture Library, 6

The British Museum, 8, 26

Giraudon/Art Resource, NY, 5 (top), 7 (top), 10, 17, 20, 22, 23 (top), 25 (top), 30, 35, 36

© Jose Luis G. Grande, The National Audubon Society Collection/Photo Researchers, 33 (bottom)

The Griffith Institute, Ashmolean Museum, 7 (bottom), 9 (bottom, right), 12, 13 (top), 14 (top)

Erich Lessing/Art Resource, NY, 9 (bottom, left), 25 (bottom)

© Tom McHugh, The National Audubon Society Collection/Photo Researchers, 33 (top)

Photography by Egyptian Expedition, The Metropolitan Museum of Art, 9 (top)

© John G. Ross/Photo Researchers, 18 (bottom)

Scala/Art Resource, NY, 34

© Ronald Sheridan/Ancient Art & Architecture Collection, 5 (bottom), 14 (bottom), 21

© Alexander Tsiaris/Photo Researchers, 28

Werner Forman/Art Resource, NY, 13 (bottom), 23 (bottom), 32

Text

Quotations within the text are taken from the following sources listed in the bibliography:

p. 8, 9, 12, 13 Howard Carter, in H. Carter, *The Tomb of Tutankhamen*

p. 17 Giovanni Belzoni, in Hamilton-Paterson, *Mummies: Death and Life in Ancient Egypt*

p. 28 James Breasted, in Romer, *Valley of the Kings*

About the Author

Lou Eschle, a telecommunications expert and amateur historian, has long been interested in the events of the past. In fact, as a child, he spent the first money he earned on a history book. He finds that the details of lives from distant times and places can shed fascinating light on life today. This is Eschle's first book in the Lucent Books Exploring the Unknown series.